STARS OF SPORTS

NEYMAR
SOCCER MAGICIAN

by Matt Chandler

CAPSTONE PRESS
a capstone imprint

Published by Capstone Press, an imprint of Capstone
1710 Roe Crest Drive, North Mankato, Minnesota 56003
capstonepub.com

Copyright © 2026 by Capstone. All rights reserved. No part of this publication may be reproduced in whole or in part, or stored in a retrieval system, or transmitted in any form or by any means, electronic, mechanical, photocopying, recording, or otherwise, without written permission of the publisher.

SPORTS ILLUSTRATED KIDS is a trademark of ABG-SI LLC. Used with permission.

Library of Congress Cataloging-in-Publication Data is available on the Library of Congress website.
ISBN: 9798875222733 (hardcover)
ISBN: 9798875222689 (paperback)
ISBN: 9798875222696 (ebook PDF)

Summary: Neymar made his professional soccer debut at 17 years old, and it didn't take long for him to become a global superstar. Discover more about Neymar's impressive career and life in this entertaining biography.

Editorial Credits
Editor: Patrick Donnelly; Designer: Sarah Bennett; Media Researcher: Svetlana Zhurkin; Production Specialist: Tori Abraham

Image Credits
Associated Press: Agencia Estado/Werther Santana, 15, Andre Penner, 11; Getty Images: AFP/Miguel Schincariol, 27, AFP/Nelson Almeida, 9, Buda Mendes, 5, David Ramos, 16, Eurasia Sport Images/Marcio Machado, 21, Francois Nel, 28, Jeff Zelevansky, 22, Lars Baron, cover, Laurence Griffiths, 18, 19, 23, Matthias Hangst, 13, 17, Pedro Vilela, 25, Victor Moriyama, 7; Shutterstock: S_Photo, 1

Source Notes
Page 6, "I saw a 6-year-old boy . . ." Corinna Halloran, "Discover Neymar Jr's childhood in Brazil," RedBull.com, January 1, 2024, https://www.redbull.com/int-en/discovering-neymar. Accessed December 2024.

Page 7, "All my career . . ." "Betinho: The man who discovered Neymar." Prothom Alo, June 1, 2018, https://en.prothomalo.com/sports/Betinho-The-man-who-discovered-Neymar. Accessed December 2024.

Page 7, "Mum, it's OK . . ." Nathan Salt, "'One day I will buy a cookie factory and eat whenever I want': Neymar reveals struggles growing up and how lack of food and money drove him to become a successful footballer." Daily Mail, December 22, 2018, https://www.dailymail.co.uk/sport/football/article-6522551/Neymar-reveals-lack-food-money-drove-successful-footballer.html. Accessed December 2024.

Page 8, "It definitely helped me . . ." Marcus Alves, "Neymar Jr on futsal, street football and tricks." FourFourTwo, September 13, 2016, https://www.fourfourtwo.com/performance/training/neymar-jr-futsal-street-football-and-tricks. Accessed December 2024.

Page 10, "We created an entirely new category . . ." Clint Smith, "Inside the unstoppable greatness of Neymar." Bleacher Report, June 7, 2018, https://mag.bleacherreport.com/neymar-brazil-world-cup-2018-larger-than-life/. Accessed December 2024.

Page 12, "We can't say . . ." Alberto Rubio, "Neymar: 10 moments in 10 years." Marca, July 3, 2019, https://www.marca.com/en/football/international-football/2019/03/07/5c81920b468aeb49588b4573.html. Accessed December 2024.

Page 27, "It makes me really happy . . ." Dermot Corrigan, "Neymar uses charity as motivation to win more trophies for Barcelona." ESPN.com, March 8, 2016, https://www.espn.com/soccer/story/_/id/37459132/neymar-uses-charity-work-motivation-win-more-trophies. Accessed December 2024.

Any additional websites and resources referenced in this book are not maintained, authorized, or sponsored by Capstone. All product and company names are trademarks™ or registered® trademarks of their respective holders.

Printed and bound in China.   006276

TABLE OF CONTENTS

RECORD SETTER 4

CHAPTER ONE
PASSION FOR THE PITCH 6

CHAPTER TWO
TIME TO GO PRO 12

CHAPTER THREE
CLUB KING 16

CHAPTER FOUR
INTERNATIONAL SUPERSTAR 22

CHAPTER FIVE
LIFE BEYOND THE PITCH 26

TIMELINE. 29
GLOSSARY. 30
READ MORE. 31
INTERNET SITES 31
INDEX 32

Words in **BOLD** are in the glossary.

RECORD SETTER

More than 52,000 fans packed Maracanã Stadium in Rio de Janeiro, Brazil. They were ready to watch Brazil take on rival Honduras. The match was a semifinal at the 2016 Olympic Games. The winner would play for the gold medal. Thanks to superstar midfielder Neymar, Brazil got off to a great start.

Honduras took possession and set up in its own end. Neymar stalked the ball and blocked a rival pass. After the steal, Neymar squared off against the goalkeeper. Neymar fired a shot just as the sliding goalkeeper took his legs out. As Neymar tumbled to the ground, the ball rolled into the net. Neymar's goal, just 14 seconds into the match, was the fastest in Olympic history. It also set the tone as Brazil crushed Honduras 6–0.

FACT

Neymar was injured on the play. He had to be taken from the field on a stretcher. He returned later in the game to score a second goal.

»»» Neymar gets taken out by the Honduras goalkeeper while scoring the first goal of Brazil's 6–0 victory in the 2016 Olympics.

CHAPTER ONE
PASSION FOR THE PITCH

Neymar da Silva Santos Jr. was born on February 5, 1992. He grew up in Praia Grande, a small town in Brazil, South America. His mother, Nadine, was one of his biggest supporters. His father, Neymar da Silva Santos Sr., also was a soccer player. Neymar has a younger sister, Rafaella, who he calls his best friend.

Like most children in his country, Neymar began playing soccer—known as *football* in Brazil—at an early age. When he was only 3 years old, he was already skilled with the ball. His first coach knew he was going to be special on the **pitch**.

"I saw a 6-year-old boy running through the stands and that caught my attention, for seeing his ability, agility, and motor coordination," the coach, Betinho Talentos, said. He approached Neymar's parents with an offer to train their son. They accepted.

⟩⟩⟩ Children play soccer on the streets of Neymar's former neighborhood in Praia Grande.

"All my career I wanted to find a player who could summon up the spirit of Pelé," Betinho said of the Brazilian superstar. "Lightning struck twice for me."

Hungry for Success

When Neymar was a child, his family had little money. His dad described their neighborhood as the place where "the entire city threw their garbage." The family was forced to move in with Neymar's grandmother. Neymar shared a mattress with his entire family. At times he wondered if he would have enough food to eat. Once, Neymar wanted cookies. His mom had to explain they had no money for cookies. Neymar was sad, but he was determined.

"Mum, it's OK. One day I will be very rich," young Neymar told his mother. "I'll buy a cookie factory so I can eat whenever I want."

FLASHES OF GREATNESS

Neymar began playing a game called futsal as a child. This five-on-five version of soccer is played on smaller surfaces. Neymar says playing in tighter spaces helped him improve his footwork.

"It definitely helped me to develop a fast game and that Brazilian smartness," he said in a 2016 interview. "I can still remember waking up every morning just wanting to play football—even though I knew I had to go to school."

When it was time to take his game to the soccer pitch, Neymar joined the Portuguesa Santista youth club in 1999. By 2004, Neymar was a star for Portuguesa Santista. He quickly developed his fast feet and blazing speed to beat defenders. He also showed his ability to score from all over the pitch.

》》》 Futsal is a fun game that helps build soccer skills.

SCOUTS TAKE NOTICE

While playing for Portuguesa Santista, Neymar was scouted by the coaches at Santos FC. Santos is one of Brazil's oldest and most successful clubs.

Neymar was only 11 years old. Santos's first level began at age 15. That didn't stop the team from signing the future star. "We created an entirely new category so Neymar could play," Brazilian soccer legend Lima said.

Neymar played for the Santos youth club for six seasons. He often faced faster and bigger players. The level of competition drove him to practice hard. Neymar soon became one of the top players in the league. His speed and ball skills were already **elite**.

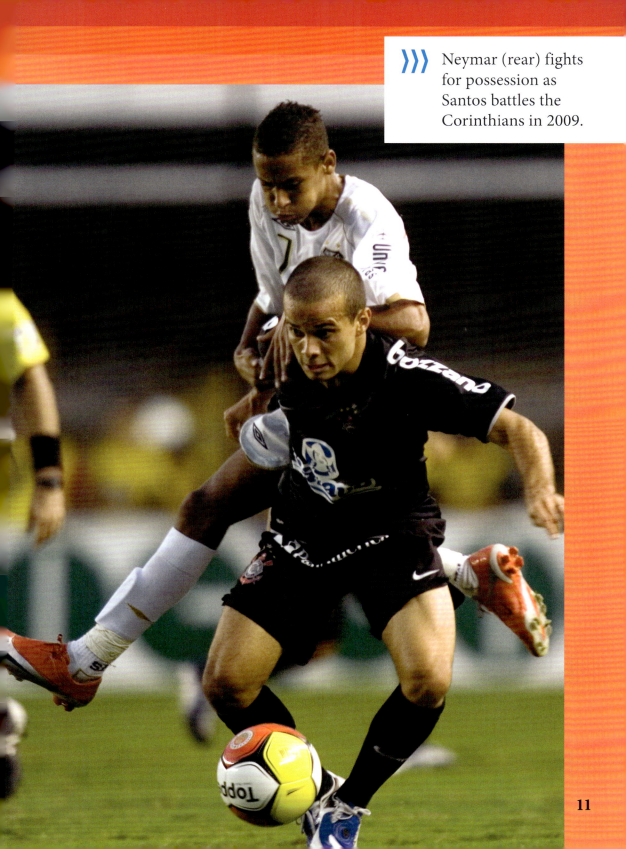

Neymar (rear) fights for possession as Santos battles the Corinthians in 2009.

CHAPTER TWO
TIME TO GO PRO

On March 7, 2009, a 17-year-old Neymar jogged onto the pitch at Pacaembu Stadium in São Paulo. Nearly 22,000 fans chanted his name. It was the second half, and Santos FC was battling Oeste de Itápolis in a scoreless match.

The Santos coaches hoped the teen would give the team a spark. It worked. Early on, Neymar rocketed a shot off the crossbar. Although he didn't find the back of the net, his play sparked Santos. The team struck twice for a 2–1 victory in Neymar's debut.

After the match, Santos coach Vagner Mancini warned fans not to compare Neymar to Brazil's greatest players after a single appearance.

"We can't say that Neymar is going to be the new Robinho or the new Pelé," Mancini said. "We must have patience."

》》》 Neymar lies on the pitch during a 2018 World Cup match against Mexico.

Growing Pains

Professional soccer players are role models for young fans. At times, Neymar has struggled to set a good example on the pitch. He often argues with officials. He has fought other players. He even headbutted an opponent while playing for Brazil.

His coaches and teammates say he has matured in recent years. But Neymar still has one bad habit on the pitch: He often falls to the ground, seemingly in pain after minor contact with an opponent. Many people think he's faking the injuries. The tactic breaks the other team's **momentum**.

SUPERSTAR ON THE PITCH

Neymar was a star when he arrived at Santos. But his talent was raw. Over the next few seasons, he grew into the player his first coaches knew he would become.

In his first full season, Neymar helped lead Santos to the **coveted** Copa do Brasil tournament. In doing so, he had one of the best matches of his young career.

Santos was taking on Guarani FC. Just two minutes in, Neymar scored on a penalty kick. It was the start of an incredible night. He added two more goals before halftime.

After yet another goal late in the game, Neymar capped his night with a beauty. He broke up the middle, streaking toward the Guarani net. Taking a pass, Neymar split two defenders. Then he ripped a low shot past the goalkeeper. Neymar's five goals highlighted an 8–1 win for Santos.

FACT

Neymar scored three goals to lead Brazil to the silver medal at the 2012 Summer Olympics.

>>> Neymar, pictured in 2010, holds two of the many trophies he's won during his career.

CHAPTER THREE
CLUB KING

In 2013, Neymar made the jump to FC Barcelona in Spain. Barcelona paid a **transfer fee** of more than 86 million euros to land Neymar. Playing alongside superstar Lionel Messi, Neymar helped Barcelona win Spain's Copa Del Rey tournament three years in a row.

Neymar's best year with Barcelona came in the 2014–15 season. He led the team to the European Champions League final. He **dominated** the tournament, leading all scorers with 10 goals.

》》》 Neymar (back row, left) and his Barcelona teammates before a 2013 match

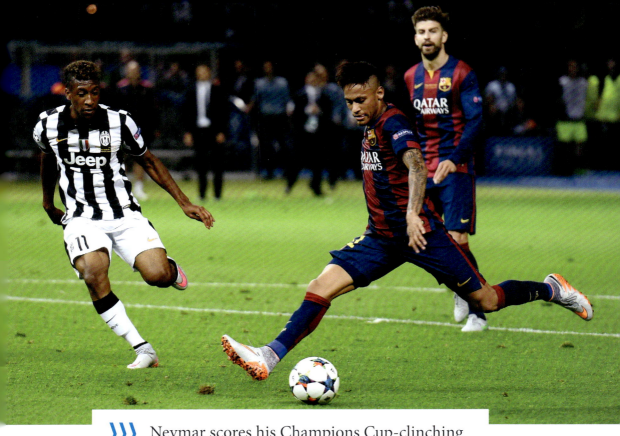

》》》 Neymar scores his Champions Cup-clinching goal against Juventus on June 6, 2015.

On June 6 , 2015, in Berlin, Germany, Barcelona faced Italy's Juventus for the Champions Cup. Late in the match, Barcelona clung to a 2–1 lead. Then Neymar crushed any hope of a Juventus comeback. The speedy star raced down the pitch and took a pass. Neymar crushed a low, left-footed shot into the net. Then he ripped off his shirt and raced to the stands to celebrate with the fans. Barcelona had captured the title.

THE KING OF SPAIN

In four seasons with Barcelona, Neymar delivered eight trophies. In 2015, Barcelona won a rare treble. That means they won three big competitions in one season. In addition to the European Champions League title, Barcelona took home the Catalan Super Cup and the Copa Del Rey.

⟩⟩⟩ Neymar celebrates after beating Juventus in the UEFA Champions League final in 2015.

The 2017 Champions League featured one of the biggest comebacks in tournament history. Barcelona faced Paris Saint-Germain (PSG) in a two-leg match. The total score of both matches would determine the winner. PSG won the first leg 4–0. Barcelona had to win the second match by five goals to advance.

Neymar and his teammates delivered. He scored on a penalty kick goal to close the gap to 5–4 in favor of PSG. Then the superstar went back-to-back. Neymar converted another crucial penalty kick goal to tie the match at 5–5. Neymar wasn't done. With seven PSG defenders in front of him, he lofted a high pass through the crowd. Teammate Sergi Roberto slid and knocked the ball in for the game winner. Neymar's two goals and the game-winning assist capped the greatest comeback in Barcelona history.

》》》 Neymar scores on a penalty kick to tie the Champions League match against PSG in 2017.

PARIS POWERHOUSE

Later that year, Neymar decided to play for PSG. The club paid a transfer fee of 222 million euros to FC Barcelona. PSG signed Neymar to a five-year contract that paid the superstar 30 million euros per year.

Neymar proved he was worth the money. In his first season with PSG, he had 19 goals and 13 assists in 20 league matches.

Neymar has collected 21 **hat tricks** in his pro career. One of his biggest came on October 3, 2018, against Red Star Belgrade in a Champions League matchup. In the 20th minute, he blasted a free kick into the top left corner of the net. Two minutes later, Neymar struck again. He raced across the middle and took a perfect pass from teammate Kylian Mbappé. Then he ripped it over the leaping goalkeeper for his second goal. In the 81st minute, Neymar completed the hat trick. PSG cruised to a 6–1 win.

Despite his success with PSG, Neymar missed 136 games due to injury. He broke bones, tore **ligaments**, and missed time with injured ribs and even COVID-19.

⟫⟫⟫ Neymar celebrates scoring a hat trick for PSG in 2022.

FACT

Neymar led PSG to five French championships in his six seasons with the club.

CHAPTER FOUR
INTERNATIONAL SUPERSTAR

Neymar was just 18 years old when he stepped onto the pitch on August 10, 2010. Brazil was facing the United States in a **friendly**. It was Neymar's first international match, and he delivered. With the match scoreless in the 28th minute, Neymar struck. A teammate passed the ball across the field. Neymar got his head on the ball. It slipped past U.S. goalkeeper Tim Howard to give Brazil the lead.

›› Neymar (11) reacts after scoring against the United States in his first international match in 2010.

Neymar went on to lead Brazil to the 2013 Confederations Cup. He scored four goals and added two assists in the tournament.

In 128 matches for Brazil's national team, Neymar has scored 79 goals. In the 2012 and 2016 Olympic Games alone, he scored seven goals in 12 matches for Brazil.

》》》 Neymar scores the Olympic gold medal-winning penalty kick against Germany in 2016.

Hometown Hero

The only thrill bigger than winning an Olympic gold medal might be to do it in your home country. When Rio de Janeiro hosted the 2016 Games, Neymar put on a show for his fellow Brazilians.

As Brazil's captain, Neymar led his team to the gold-medal game and a chance at history. The score was tied after 120 minutes. It would be decided by penalty kicks. It all came down to Neymar. The superstar lined up his kick. He got German goaltender Timo Horn off-balance with a little stutter step. Then, he ripped a low, hard shot into the back of the net. Neymar did it! Brazil had its gold medal.

HIGHS AND LOWS

Picking the greatest highlight from Neymar's incredible career is a difficult task. But in Brazil, scoring more goals than national hero Pelé is a solid choice.

Brazil was taking on Bolivia in a World Cup qualifier match in 2023. Neymar had tied Pelé's record of 77 international goals earlier in the match. With Brazil ahead 3–0, Neymar made history. He picked up a loose ball in front of the Bolivia goal. Then he drove it into the back of the net. The crowd went wild as Neymar celebrated his place as Brazil's all-time leading international scorer.

With the highs come the lows. Many critics point out that Neymar has never led Brazil to a World Cup championship. Pelé led Brazil to World Cup victories in 1958, 1962, and 1970.

Neymar was honored after he broke Pelé's scoring record for Brazil in 2023.

FACT

In August 2023, Neymar signed with Al-Hilal SFC of the Saudi Pro League. After just five matches, he suffered a season-ending injury. With Neymar out, the club won the 2023–24 Saudi Arabian championship.

CHAPTER FIVE
LIFE BEYOND THE PITCH

Neymar is more than just one of the greatest soccer players in the world. He is also a worldwide celebrity. Neymar earns more than $28 million each year **endorsing** products. The superstar has deals with Puma, Red Bull, Beats Electronics, and Gillette, among others.

He is also one of the most popular athletes on social media. Neymar has 225 million followers on Instagram.

Neymar uses his celebrity status to give back all over the world. He started the Neymar Jr. Institute in São Paulo, Brazil. The project gives thousands of children educational and sports opportunities.

>>> Neymar speaks with reporters during a 2024 charity auction at the Neymar Jr. Institute.

"It makes me really happy to do something for these kids and their families," Neymar said.

He also donated $1 million to help fight the COVID-19 **pandemic** in Brazil.

G.O.A.T.?

Neymar has built an incredible career on the pitch. He has become a world-famous celebrity. Still, there is a lot of **debate** among soccer fans. Will Neymar go down as the greatest to ever play the game? He faces stiff competition. Lionel Messi is a 10-time La Liga Champion. Cristiano Ronaldo has scored more international goals than anyone in history. Fellow Brazilian Pelé tallied more than 1,200 career goals.

It may be impossible to say who is the true G.O.A.T. But there is no question that Neymar is one of the most talented players ever.

》》》 Neymar chases the ball for Al Hilal during a Saudi Pro League match in 2023.

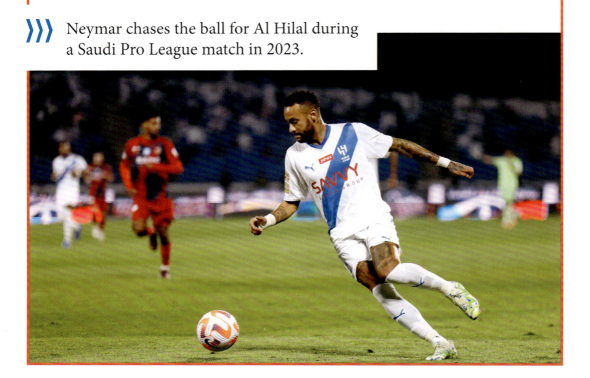

TIMELINE

1992 — Neymar da Silva Jr. is born on February 5 in Brazil.

1999 — Neymar begins his youth career by signing with Portuguesa Santista.

2003 — Neymar signs with the Santos FC youth team.

2009 — On October 24, Neymar joins the Brazil U17 squad to begin his international career.

2011 — Neymar is named "Footballer of the Year" for Brazil.

2015 — On June 6, Neymar wins the European Champions League title with Barcelona.

2016 — At the Summer Olympics in Rio de Janeiro, Brazil, Neymar converts the game-winning penalty kick to secure the gold medal.

2023 — Neymar scores his 78th goal for Brazil, breaking the national record held by soccer legend Pelé.

FACT

In 2022, Neymar became only the third player in history to score 100 goals with three different clubs. He scored 136 with Santos, 105 with Barcelona, and 118 with PSG.

GLOSSARY

COVETED (CUV-uht-uhd)—very popular or desired by many

DEBATE (duh-BAYT)—discussion designed to present opposing sides of an issue

DOMINATED (DOM-in-ayt-uhd)—took control of

ELITE (uh-LEET)—the best of the best

ENDORSING (en-DOOR-sing)—declaring one's support of a product or person

FRIENDLY (FREND-lee)—a match that is not part of league play or a tournament; an exhibition

HAT TRICK (HAT TRIK)—three goals scored by one player in the same game

LIGAMENT (LIG-uh-muhnt)—tissue that connects bones to stabilize joints

MOMENTUM (mow-MEN-tuhm)—strength or positive feelings gained by a series of events

PANDEMIC (pan-DEM-ick)—a disease spreading rapidly through a population

PITCH (PITCH)—another term for a soccer field

TRANSFER FEE (TRANZ-fuhr FEE)—an amount of money sent from one club to another when a player changes teams

READ MORE

Berglund, Bruce. *Soccer GOATs: The Greatest Athletes of All Time.* North Mankato, MN: Capstone, 2024.

Hunter, Nick. *Soccer Record Breakers.* North Mankato, MN: Capstone, 2025.

Keith, Tanya. *Soccer Biographies for Kids.* Naperville, IL: Callisto Kids, 2024.

INTERNET SITES

Biography: Neymar
biography.com/athletes/neymar

FC Barcelona: Neymar Da Silva
fcbarcelona.com/en/card/3925551/neymar-da-silva

Neymar Jr.
neymarjr.com

INDEX

Arantes do Nascimento, Edson (Pelé), 7, 12, 24, 25, 28, 29

Brazil, South America, 4, 5, 6, 10, 12, 13, 14, 22, 23, 24, 25, 26, 27, 29

COVID-19 pandemic, 20, 27

Da Silva Santos, Neymar, Sr., 6, 7

endorsements, 26
European Champions League, 16, 18, 19, 20, 29

FC Barcelona, 16, 17, 18, 19, 20, 29

injuries, 13, 20, 25

Neymar Jr. Institute, 26, 27

Olympics, 4, 5, 14, 23, 29

Paris Saint-Germain (PSG), 19, 20, 21, 29
penalty kicks, 14, 19, 23, 29
Portuguesa Santista, 8, 10, 29

Santos FC, 10, 11, 12, 14, 29
stadiums, 4, 12

Talentos, Betinho, 6, 7

World Cup, 13, 24

AUTHOR BIO

Matt Chandler is the author of more than 60 books for children and thousands of articles published in newspapers and magazines. He writes mostly nonfiction books with a focus on sports, ghosts and haunted places, and graphic novels. Matt lives in New York.